What Happens When We Recycle

Food and Garden Waste?

Jillian Powell

FRANKLIN WATTS
LONDON·SYDNEY

First published in 2009 by Franklin Watts
338 Euston Road, London NW1 3BH

Franklin Watts Australia
Level 17/207 Kent Street
Sydney NSW 2000

Editor: Julia Bird
Designer: DR Ink
Art Director: Jonathan Hair

Picture credits: Donald Barger/Shutterstock:front cover br,
11, 27b; Alex Bartel/Ecoscene: 21; Ian Beames/Ecoscene:
12; Mark Boulton/Alamy: 23; John Boykin/Alamy: 15;
Byogy Renewables Inc.: 16; Sebastian Cote/Istockphoto:
27t; Tom Ennis/Ecoscene: 9; Envision/Corbis: 24.
Greenshoots Communications/Alamy: 22; Angela
Hampton/Ecoscene: 25tr; Ian Harwood/Ecoscene:
14, 27c; Radomir Jirsak/Shutterstock: 7;
Kokhanchikov/Shutterstock: 19; Roy Langstaff/Ecoscene:
13; Ellen McKnight/Alamy: 25bl; Nic Murray/Alamy:
front cover t; Photoroller/Shutterstock: 17;
Proteus/Waste Watch: 18; Shutterlist/Shutterstock: 6.
Don Smith/Alamy: front cover bl; Waste Watch: 8.
Wrap/Waste Watch: 10.

A CIP catalogue record for this book
is available from the British Library

ISBN: 978 0 7496 8185 2

Dewey Classification: 363.72'88

Printed in China

Franklin Watts is a division of
Hachette Children's Books,
an Hachette Livre UK company.
www.hachettelivre.co.uk

Contents

Organic waste

Food scraps like these can be recycled.

Household waste

Every day, we throw away millions of tonnes of household rubbish. About a third of the contents of our dustbins is kitchen or garden waste.

Kitchen and garden waste

Kitchen waste includes food scraps, vegetable and fruit peelings, egg shells and tea bags. Garden waste includes weeds and dead flowers, leaves, twigs, branches and cut grass.

● Biodegradable

Food and garden waste is often sent to **landfill sites**, but it is better to recycle it as it is **organic**. Organic waste is **biodegradable** which means that it will break down naturally, unlike glass, plastics and metal waste.

DID YOU KNOW?

- In the UK we throw away 6.7 million tonnes of food each year – about a third of all the food we buy.

Organic material like this dead tree biodegrades naturally in woodland.

Why recycle food and garden waste?

● Landfill

There are several reasons why we should recycle organic waste. Every year, millions of tonnes of food and garden waste are dumped on landfill sites. In landfill, organic waste **rots** underground. It produces **methane**, which is a **greenhouse gas**. It also produces a smelly liquid called **leachate** which **pollutes** land, lakes and rivers.

Refuse lorries dump rubbish on landfill sites. The rubbish is then buried.

The environment

Recycled organic waste can be used to make **compost**. Compost feeds the soil so it reduces the need for chemical **fertilisers** which can harm the **environment**. Using compost also reduces the amount of water needed to grow crops.

Peat bogs

Using compost reduces the use of **peat**. Peat is an organic material that is used to improve soil for farming and gardening. Peat **bogs** need to be protected because they are important habitats for plants and animals.

Peat bogs are home to rare animals and plants.

Making compost

Good for plants

Compost improves soil because it contains goodness from rotted plants and food. It can be made at home in your garden, in a **wormery** or at a recycling plant.

Greens and browns

Compost needs a mix of 'greens' such as fruit and vegetable peelings and grass, and 'browns' such as twigs, leaves, paper and card. It can be made in heaps in the open air, in closed bins or in giant drums called **bio vessels**.

It is important to get the right mix of ingredients to make good compost.

Micro-organisms

First, the waste begins to biodegrade as **micro-organisms** feed off the greens. The **energy** they create heats the waste up and more micro-organisms and **moulds** start to grow in it.

Minibeasts

As the waste cools, **fungi** grow and minibeasts such as slugs, worms and beetles begin to break down the browns. After a few months, the waste has rotted into compost. It is no longer smelly and is like crumbly soil.

?

DID YOU KNOW?

A worm eats and digests half its body weight in waste every day.

This handful of compost is ready to use.

Collection

● Collecting food waste

Householders can send food and garden waste away to be turned into compost. Food waste can be collected from homes in biodegradable bags or small plastic bins with lids. Recycling lorries also collect food waste from businesses, restaurants and supermarkets.

GREEN GUIDE

Kitchen waste such as cooked meat or fish bones can be smelly. It should be wrapped in newspaper before it is put in the recycling bin. This stops the smell attracting pests like flies, rats or foxes.

Garden waste

Garden waste is collected from homes, parks and gardens in biodegradable sacks or brown wheelie bins. Some households need to buy special sacks or bins to put their garden waste in.

Garden waste includes grass clippings, dead branches, weeds and fallen leaves.

Recycling plants

Lorries take the waste to special recycling plants where it will be stored and turned into compost. At recycling plants, machines use different methods to speed up the time it takes to turn waste into compost.

Sorting and shredding

At the recycling plant

Once the waste has been delivered to the recycling plant, it needs to be cleaned. Kitchen waste can have food packaging mixed in with it. Garden waste can include bits of rock, broken glass or metal. These all have to be removed or they could spoil the compost.

GREEN GUIDE

Paper and cardboard are biodegradable and will rot as compost, but glass, metals and some types of plastic are non-biodegradable.

Hand or machine?

At some plants, the waste is cleaned on **conveyor belts.** Workers pick out any bits of rubbish like plastics, glass, stones or metals by hand. Other plants have machines that sort the waste and remove any unwanted rubbish. Machines use **screens**, **magnets** and de-stoners to remove rubbish.

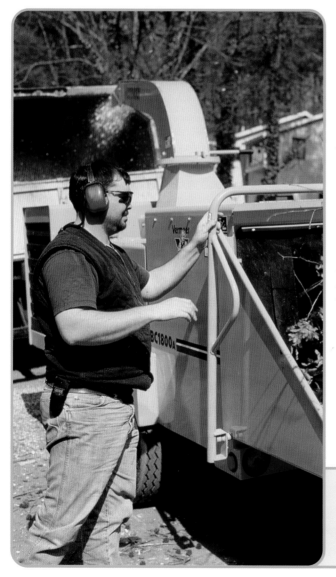

Shredding

Trees and other woody garden waste go into giant shredding machines. These chop the waste into small pieces. This helps to speed up the composting process.

Workers should protect their eyes and ears when using shredding machines.

15

Food waste

Mixing

Cleaned food waste can be recycled into compost on its own. It can also be mixed with other biodegradable waste such as garden waste and cardboard. At the recycling plant, the waste is loaded into bio vessels.

Bio vessels

The bio vessels mix up the waste. Inside, the vessels are heated to around 70 degrees Celsius. This kills any **germs** and speeds up composting.

Bio vessels can be linked to computers that tell them when to turn the waste to control the temperature.

● Screening

The waste passes from one part of the bio vessel to the next as it rots down. After three weeks, it is ready to be taken out. The waste is then stored in long heaps called **windrows**. These are left for up to 12 weeks. The waste is then ready to be used as compost.

Windrows laid out at a green waste recycling plant.

Meat and fish waste

Germs

Animal food scraps like meat and fish bones can contain germs, so they must be composted separately. Dumper trucks unload the waste at recycling plants, which are often on farms. The waste is sieved first so that any small bits drop through. Bigger bits are shredded, then the waste is piled into windrows.

Heating up

The windrows are turned to keep them moist. The heat that builds up inside them kills germs and fungi. Bulldozers then move the waste into piles where they are left to rot down further.

The piles of rotted food waste heat up as micro-organisms feed off the waste.

Drying

Sometimes animal food waste is dried to prepare it for composting. The waste is fed into a machine which shreds and dries it with hot air. The heat kills any germs and nasty smells. The waste turns into a dry powder, which is collected by lorries and taken for composting in bio vessels or a wormery.

JUST THE FACTS

Some food driers can compost up to 2,000 kilograms of food waste a day.

Worms make compost by digesting organic waste in a wormery.

New products: food

Biogas

Another way of re-using food waste is to make a **renewable** source of energy called **biogas**. Biogas plants can use cooked or uncooked food waste, including meat and bones.

Digesters

Food waste is sent to the plant from household food bins, restaurants and food processing factories. The food is mashed up and heated in huge **digesters** that contain no air. As it heats up, micro-organisms begin to feed and break the waste down.

These digesters break down organic waste without air.

Energy and fertilisers

The digesters turn the waste into biogas and liquid or solid waste called **digestate**. The biogas is used to drive an engine that creates heat and electricity. Some of the heat is used again at the biogas plant. The digestate is used as a fertiliser. The electricity can be used for many different purposes.

DID YOU KNOW? ?

Biogas factories can also use plant crops and animal manure to make biogas.

This train in Sweden runs on biogas. It is the world's first biogas train.

Garden waste

Unloading

Garden waste can be composted outside. Lorries unload the shredded waste into windrows. As micro-organisms begin to break down the waste, the windrows heat up inside. Machines suck and blow air through them, helping to speed up the composting.

?

DID YOU KNOW?

The garden waste that goes to landfill each year could fill the Royal Albert Hall in London more than 70 times!

This dumper truck is unloading shredded green waste on a farm where it will be composted.

Adding air

The windrows are regularly turned and mixed by hand or by digger or turning machines. This helps to put air into the mix. It can take weeks or even months for the compost to be ready to use.

Screening

When the compost is ready, it passes through screens to remove any bits of rubbish that have not rotted down. The compost can then be bagged up ready for use.

These sacks of compost are for sale at a garden centre.

New products: garden waste

● Products

As well as compost, garden waste can also be turned into **soil conditioner** or **mulch**. Tree waste can be recycled as timber, firewood or chippings.

This high-quality compost is being used for mushroom farming.

● Compost quality

There are different grades of compost. The best is used to improve the soil on farms. Lower grades can have tiny bits of plastic or other waste mixed in. They can be used in parks and gardens. Soil conditioner improves soil by feeding it and helping it to hold in moisture.

Mulch

Wood or bark from trees can be turned into chippings and used as mulch. Mulch covers and protects soil. It keeps garden borders tidy and helps to hold in moisture and stop weeds growing.

Mulch can protect young plants against pests.

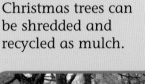

Christmas trees can be shredded and recycled as mulch.

GREEN GUIDE

Over 6 million fir trees are sold at Christmas in the UK. Many go to landfill after Christmas, creating over 9,000 tonnes of green waste! There are collections and recycling centres for Christmas trees all over the UK, so check with your local council.

What you can do

Pupils at Catherine McAuley School in Ireland run their own composting scheme. They keep kitchen caddies on each corridor and one class is in charge of collecting and emptying them into the compost bins in the school garden each week. Pupils work as members of The Green School Committee wearing green gloves and bibs. They collect all the leftovers from school lunches and cookery classes, as well as leaves and garden waste from the school grounds.

5 top tips for food and garden waste recyclers:

1 Use gloves when handling waste.

2 Wrap food in newspaper, not plastic.

3 Recycle meat, fish or cooked food separately.

4 Remove all packaging before recycling food.

5 Make your own compost at home if you can.

Making compost

You will need:

A compost bin
Green waste (fruit and
vegetable peelings, grass)

Brown waste (twigs, paper,
cardboard)
An adult to help

Step 1
Cover the bottom of the bin with a layer of earth.

Step 2
Start adding the waste, mixing layers of greens and browns.

Step 3
Every now and then, add layers of scrunched up or shredded newspaper or card.

Step 4
Open the compost to the air on dry days.

Step 5
Fork through the compost from time to time.

Step 6
When the compost looks like crumbly brown soil, it is ready to use.

Glossary

Biodegradable   Able to break down naturally.

Biogas   A type of gas that contains methane and carbon dioxide and can be used to make electricity.

Bio vessels   Giant containers for composting organic waste.

Compost   Earthy material that forms when organic matter rots down.

Conveyor belts   Moving belts which transport things, for example through a recycling plant or factory.

Digestate   Solid or liquid fertiliser produced by digesters.

Digesters   Containers used for breaking down organic waste.

Energy   Heat or power.

Environment   Surroundings.

Fertiliser   A substance made from chemicals, manure or compost that is used to improve soil.

Fungi   Type of plants, including moulds and mushrooms, that feed on organic matter.

Germs   Tiny living things that can cause illness or disease.

Greenhouse gas   A gas that traps heat in the Earth's atmosphere and contributes to global warming.

Landfill sites   Places where rubbish is buried under the ground.

Leachate   Smelly liquid waste.

Magnets   Pieces of metal that can draw metals containing iron towards them.

Methane   A kind of gas that can cause global warming.

Micro-organisms   Tiny living things.

Moulds   Fungi and other organisms that grow on rotting matter.

Mulch   A covering for soil.

Organic   To do with living things, such as plants, fruits and vegetables.

Peat   A rich and increasingly rare organic material found in marshy areas.

Peat bogs   Marshy land where peat is found.

Pollute   To make dirty.

Renewable   Able to be renewed and so will not run out.

Rot   To break down.

Screens   Sieves.

Soil conditioner   A soil improver that provides food and helps it to hold in moisture.

Windrows   Long rows or heaps.

Wormery   A container for composting organic matter with the help of worms.

Further information

Books

Composting: Nature's Recyclers (Amazing Science), Robin Michal
Koontz and Matthew Harrad, Picture Window Books 2006

Minibeasts On a Compost Heap (Where To Find Minibeasts),
Sarah Ridley, Franklin Watts 2008

What's Going on in the Compost Pile? (A Book About Systems),
Rachel Chappell, Rourke Publishing 2008

Websites

www.recyclenow.com/home_composting/index.html
Detailed information on composting at home.

www.wasteonline.org.uk
Information on recycling all kinds of waste, including composting.

www.recyclezone.org.uk
Lots of information on recycling, with sections on composting and
worms and setting up a school compost scheme.

Note to parents and teachers: Every effort has been made by the Publishers
to ensure that the websites in this book are suitable for children, that they
are of the highest educational value, and that they contain no
inappropriate or offensive material. However, because of the nature of the
Internet, it is impossible to guarantee that the contents of these sites will not
be altered. We strongly advise that Internet access is supervised by a
responsible adult.

Index